Gambling

The Pleasure of Winning, the Pain of Losing
"Women Living Through the Pain"

L. LYNN HILLIARD

Copyright © 2011 by L. Lynn Hilliard
Los Angeles, California
All Rights Reserved

Printed and Bound in the United States of America

Published and Distributed by:
Professional Publishing House
1424 W. Manchester Ave., Suite B
Los Angeles, CA 90047
www.professionalpublishinghouse.com
Drrosie@aol.com
323-750-3592

Cover Design: M&A Media
Interior Design: Caldonia Joyce
              Visual Bridge Designs

First Printing, June 2011
10 9 8 7 6 5 4 3 2 1
ISBN 978-0-9834444-1-1

Publisher's Note
All rights reserved. No part of this book may be reproduced in whole or in part, in any form or by any means, electronic or mechanical, including photocopying, recording or by any information storage and retrieval system, without permission in writing from the author. Address inquiries to: L. Lynn Hilliard at Reformedfromgambling@verizon.net

ACKNOWLEGEMENTS

I want to thank God Almighty, who gave me the strength and knowledge to write this book. I submit to you for I can do nothing without you. I give all praise to you God for my life, restoration and my ability to tell this story. For every problem there is an answer, and I commit to you God, the problem solver and the deliverer.

I have so much appreciation for my spiritual leader, my pastor, and my friend, Pastor Charles E. Lollis, for all your support and guidance. It is from your teaching that I am assured that I am okay with God. He loves me unconditionally, and He is a forgiving and a restoring God, Thank you.

I thank my three sons, my husband, my brother, cousins and other family members and friends for their patience, understanding, and support and for putting up with my craziness, during this birthing process. You are symbolic of God's unconditional love that has carried me through the evolution of being redeemed, from my addiction.

ABOUT THE AUTHOR

L. Lynn Hilliard is a native of Chicago Illinois. Now residing in southern California, she is a prolific and profound life application writer. Hilliard holds a street degree in Professional Gambling and conducts session on dealing with relationships, finances, stress management and the spiritual warfare of gambling.

Today Hilliard has climbed the ladder of personal success and now uses those learning experiences as priceless tools for empowering others to excel beyond the bondage of physical, emotional and mental boundaries in their addiction.

DEDICATION

This book is dedicated to the memory of my cousin, Helen L. Harding, who encouraged me, talked to me, and typed for me. When I got on her nerves, she would lovingly "go on strike" against me, but only for a couple of hours. She constantly reminded me that this is the only child that I could create to be what I want. Cousin, I am saddened that you did not get to see this birth to the end. Your support and love meant so much to me. I miss you more than anyone knows. You showed me just how special and highly favored by God you were by being born and meeting our maker on the same day, May 10, 1943 – May 10, 2010.

Thank you for allowing Kathy into my life—the daughter I never had. Our bond is closer than I could ever imagine.

To the loves of my life, my parents Ernest and Helen Harper, who stood by me through thick and thin. I love you and miss you so much. I regret that my world of addiction brought you so much pain. My only wish is that you could have lived to see the changes in my life. I thank you so much for your unconditional love and support. Through our faith in God, we will meet again and I know he will greet me in the same manner and say, "Well Done My Loyal and Faithful Servant. Job Well Done".

SPECIAL THANKS

To my special friend of forty-three years, Reginald G. Shikami, words could never express how you have touched my life. Thank you for having faith in me to accomplish any adventure that I set out to achieve, and your foresight of seeing in me the wisdom that I never knew existed. Thank you for your mental support, guidance and encouragement through the many years.

To my cousin Kathleen Marie Harding Grace, you represent the true meaning of family. I appreciate you and thank you so very much for taking time out of your busy schedule to help me. I truly couldn't have done it without you. Your love, support and faith in my project means so much to me.

Last, but not least, I thank you, Dr. Rosie Milligan, for your patience, dedication and understanding in helping me birth this "Book Baby". After seven years, through your inspiration and constant push my baby was finally born.

TABLE OF CONTENTS

ACKNOWLEGEMENTS		3
ABOUT THE AUTHOR		5
DEDICATION		7
SPECIAL THANKS		9
NOTE FROM THE AUTHOR		13
PREFACE		15
INTRODUCTION		17
1.	A FOOL AND A SCHOLAR	21
2.	THE FORMATIVE YEARS	24
3.	PEOPLE THAT HAVE LOST THEIR WAY	30
4.	LOVE AT FIRST SIGHT	32
5.	ALL GROWN UP	35
6.	LOOK BEFORE YOU LEAP	38
7.	A BREATH OF FRESH AIR	41
8.	NEVER FORGET YOUR ROOTS	44
9.	GAMBLING IS LONGER THAN LIFE	47
10.	ON MY OWN NOW!	51
11.	HEARTBREAK	54

TABLE OF CONTENTS

12.	THE BEGINNING AND END	57
13.	WHERE ARE THE JOBS	60
14.	HISTORY REPEATS ITSELF	63
15.	A SAD BUT SPECIAL DAY	66
16.	YAP—YAP	69
17.	FULFILLING A DREAM	72
18.	THE CLIENT LIST	76
19.	THE UPS AND DOWNS OF BUSINESS	79
20.	LOAN SHARK	81
21.	GAMBLING'S PAYOFF	84
22.	GRANNY'S PAIN	86
23.	FIRST ONE IN	90
24.	THE GAME KIDS PLAY	93
25.	THE REPORT	97
26.	THE NEWS	101
27.	ANOTHER DAY'S JOURNEY	105
28.	IF MONEY ONLY CAME WITH INSTRUCTIONS	108
29.	THE TRUST	112
30.	CLOSING DAY	119
31.	THE SHOCK OF HER LIFE	128

NOTE FROM THE AUTHOR

The names of the characters are fictitious—but the stories are inspired by real life experiences. Some of the experiences are mine, and some experiences I have seen through friends and family members that also did not recognize the addiction before it ruined their lives.

PREFACE

One of the most pathological diseases that's epidemic today is gambling addiction. The disease is a silent destroyer of one's mind, values and families.

When we think of gamblers, we usually put the face on a man; therefore, women are unsuspected victims. Women who gamble heavily are a new phenomenon. But according to recent research, women are fast surpassing men as casino customers and make up a growing number of problem gamblers.

During the cable television show on A&E, which aired a show about women compulsive gamblers on February 23, 2009, it was noted that compulsive gambling among women is a growing problem. While ten years ago only 3 percent of compulsive gamblers were women, that number is 46 percent or higher today. In the United States, about 2 million adults (1%) meet the criteria for compulsive or pathological gambling in a given year, according to the National Council on Problem Gambling (NCPG). Another 4 to 6 million (2 to 3%) can be considered problem gamblers, defined as someone who meets one or more

Preface

of the criteria and are experiencing problems because of their gambling behavior.

These women will neglect and or lose their children, husbands, homes and their jobs due to their gambling addiction. They will pawn their jewelry, car and anything of value. It is nothing for them to have 10 outstanding loans with the Pay Day Loan businesses. This mind-controlling disease has no respect of person, it matters not the social and economic status. Gambling addiction is rapidly and silently destroying the lives of too many women and their families. It is my hope that people will learn and recognize the signs and symptoms of a gambling addiction and encourage men and women alike to seek professional help before they ruin their life and the lives of their families.

INTRODUCTION

You don't know me...I am the grandmother, the mother, the daughter, the housewife, the real estate broker, the teacher, the doctor, the lawyer, the welfare recipient, the person living on a once a month pension, the person living from paycheck to paycheck. I come in all shapes, forms, and colors. I have no social or economic boundaries. I am the gambling addict; I am you, haunted by an unrealistic dream caught up in the emotions of the moment living for the pain and pleasure of gambling.

In retrospect, I reflect on the first time I placed a bet, the rush, the joy, and the pain. Coming down from my high, reality sets in. I am broke so I try again to win. One night of gambling turns into days, days into weeks, weeks into months, and months into years. I am one paycheck from bankruptcy and one mortgage payment from homelessness. Unlike substance abuse, society accepts casinos, card clubs, bingo parlors, horse racing, sports betting, lottery, all of which contribute to the legalized gambling addiction.

Gambling is an addiction so crippling it takes away your identity. Something happens when you are in a gambling environment. You feel you'll never win enough. You tell yourself "If I can get back what I've lost, I'll leave". It never happens; you

INTRODUCTION

are hooked. You leave a loser. A sucker never wins and a loser never quits.

Seven casinos exist in the county of Los Angeles, there are Indian reservations in the desert area, cable TV poker tournaments, Internet gambling, and the news media advertise free poker lessons for the beginner. Back in the day, gambling was a man's sport. Gambling has become a life sentence for the old and especially the younger generations of women. These women are losing their hard earned money, living in hotels with their children, turning to prostitution and some even contemplate suicide.

Many gamblers wonder how and why they lost everything that was important in their lives, their families, friends, integrity, sense of value and almost their minds. It is because gambling is a game of chance that has no certainty. There is no end to what you can win, but there is an end to what you can lose. We pay the least amount of bills only to save a large amount of money to place another bet. We write checks to pay bills only to use the ATM to withdraw the funds for those checks that have not yet cleared the bank. We borrow money we cannot repay, consequently dodging people we owe.

We honestly believe we will win. We are always in denial. Subconsciously, we enjoy the pleasure of winning and the pain of losing. Gambling is legal and accessible. This legal drug has the same consequences as illegal drugs; it will consume your life. It's an overwhelming addiction that has destructive effects.

We really want to stop but our desires don't equal our passion. You lie to yourself, and say you are going to quit. As soon as we get our hand on fresh money we think of a million reasons why we need to gamble. Gambling is like your non-dominant hand, we feel we need it, we can do without it, but we think we have to have it.

Gambling

Sometimes change is so complex we cannot handle change alone, we need a higher power. Unless significant changes are made, we will never end the path of self-destruction, and the hole in our soul will never be fulfilled.

Chapter 1

A Fool and a Scholar

Autumn had run out of hope; she could not help but cry. Her BMW convertible was history. The bicycle that once was used for pleasure had become her only means of transportation. Her feet blistered from the repetitive motion, her soiled clothing reeked of second hand smoke, and the lack of personal hygiene was a constant reminder of that one wrong turn that lead her on a path to self-destruction.

Nowhere to call home with less than pocket change, her heart was heavy and her spirit was weak. Feeling helpless, homeless, and hungry, her tired and cloudy eyes fought back the tears that were obstructing her view. Her throat was closing from choking on her own tears. She had no choice but to stop her two-wheeler. She cleared her throat with a sip of water and took a few deep breaths.

Behind the seat of her bicycle was a rack that once transported her puppy, it now concealed all that was left of her earthly possessions; her Bible, a blanket, her favorite portrait of herself, her great grandmother Helen and her twin sister Amber, a CD player and a CD with her favorite gospel songs, one apple, two bananas, a large bottle of water, and a bag of strawberry lollipops.

As Autumn reminisced about her past, she more than ever missed her great grandmother Helen, who was lovingly called GG by the twins. Every day she intended to call her great grandmother, but always found an excuse not to call. In reality, that silent part of her brain was ashamed. She wished she had done things differently, but it was too late. The bottom had already dropped out.

She was so far down the only way out was up. She felt as if she was in the middle of a nightmare, which she did not want to be a part of and had no ending. In her dreams, she kept trying to wake up, but something kept pulling her back.

Autumn sucked on a lollipop, as she peddled her bike to where she found refuge for the past few months—her secret place. Her torn spirit could not help reverting to her childhood. Peddling her two-wheeler to her secret hiding place, she reflected on the life she chose, the family she abandoned, and the choices she made.

The birds were silent as if not understanding the seasons. A big cloud that surrounded the glow of spring hid the sun. The climate was hot and muggy. The seasons, confused of their purpose, seemed as if they reflected all the emotions that her thoughts could not express. Through her tears, she could only smile as she remembered the days of grandeur.

Chapter 2

The Formative Years

Escaping death, as mere infants strapped in their car seats, Autumn and her twin sister, Amber, were found alive and unharmed. They survived a head on car collision that, unfortunately, claimed the lives of their parents and grandparents. After the tragedy, GG, the twin's only surviving relative, welcomed the girls with opens arms. When the girls were babies, GG converted one of three bedrooms into a nursery. The only difference was rather than visiting, it was now their home.

GG, the first generation, was proud to be a great grandmother. The twin's childhood was filled with love. GG never missed a morning or evening without giving the girls a big hug or showering them with an affectionate gesture.

Gambling

The mild-mannered little woman, with mingled grey hair and piecing grey eyes, was very clairvoyant. It always appeared as if she could read your mind. GG was raised in a holiness church. The women of the church wore very loose clothing not to reveal their figure, no makeup was worn, and they always wore hats and gloves. As Helen grew up, some of the elders in the church said, "Sister Helen, a God-fearing woman, was born with a veil over her face and seemingly had a sixth sense."

Sometimes she saw good and bad things. This could have been one of the reasons why GG never mentioned the million-dollar insurance policy that carried a double indemnity clause that was left to the twins by their parents and grandparents. GG decided that the twins twenty-sixth birthdays would be a good time to tell the twins they were millionaires. Helen was a smart woman. During the nineties, when the stock market was booming, she invested wisely allowing her to provide an affordable education for the twins without touching their inheritance.

As little girls, the twins would awake early and run to GG's room finding the door slightly cracked. They could hear GG's voice telling someone to go to hell where he belonged, but they never heard a reply. They thought that maybe their great grandmother had a man in her room. They also could not understand why GG would curse. Out of nowhere, she would begin to talk in a language they could not comprehend. The girls would look at each other very puzzled, wondering why GG talked to herself.

After GG finished talking in a foreign language, without warning, she would explode into song and laughter. GG would start singing words that sounded like, "Falling in love with J'us was the best thing I ever did." When it became apparent the conversation had stopped, the twins would run into their room and pretend they were just waking up.

They looked to see if the person GG called J'us would follow her out of the bedroom, but he never did. One day, as the girls grew more inquisitive. Amber asked GG, "Who is this J'us that you talk to every morning and why do you tell him to go back to hell where he belonged, but then you start singing to him and telling him how much you love him and that he is the best thing that has ever happened to you?" With a sad look, as if they lost their best friend, Amber asked, "Do you love J'us more then you love us?" GG replied, "Girls have a seat and I am going to tell you a story." She looked at the girls with those piercing eyes, as though she could read their thoughts. "Every morning I wake up, the first thing I do is take down the rug that hangs over my bedroom door and fall on my knees. I tell Jesus to have his way with my life today. I ask Jesus to send the devil back to hell, where he belongs. The language I speak only

Gambling

Jesus can understand. Finally, I let Jesus know he is the best thing that has ever happened to me."

The girls always lived a normal and stable life, with GG. They attended Christian school and never lived above their means. The girls looked forward to the weekends. On Saturdays they loved to run around the enormously large Members Only discount store, which had different vendors, with all kinds of foods to sample. They always came home with a bag of various-colored lollipops. GG would tell the girls no candy, but Autumn loved the strawberry lollipops so much, GG always gave in to her craving. By the time they arrived home, they were so full they could not eat another bite.

Saturdays was the only day that they did not eat dinner together. Otherwise, the family of three never missed dinner together. As they sat at the table that seated six, they would discuss worldly events and educational topics.

One evening after dinner, for no apparent reason, GG looked at the twins and said, "Some people are raised and some grow up. I always want you to remember you should never be ashamed to say I made a mistake. You should look back and say, I am not that person I used to be, nor am I the person that I want to be, but tomorrow I will try harder to strive for perfection."

They attended church services at least twice a week and every Sunday. GG never forgot the roots that were embedded in her thoughts; she was a very simple, but thoughtful, person. Sunday, Wednesday and Thursday were special days because the kids had to attend church services. GG said, "Sunday was the day to get your spiritual food that got you through the week. Wednesday was Bible study, a time to learn God's teachings, and Thursday was Pastoral night, and also a special day to give thanks and receive special blessings in case you get hungry Monday, Tuesday, Friday and Saturday."

Amber and Autumn's lives were filled with love and values. The girls had voices that complemented each other. When they sang, the sound was like two birds on a hot summer day. Their lives were filled with happiness; their spirits were free from all the displeasure of life's disappointments. It was no wonder the twins sang the lead in the little people's choir. After Sunday school, when the other children were playing, the twins would sneak off to their secret place. Mrs. Jones, who was in charge of watching over the children after Sunday school, would always fall asleep, leaving the children alone to play in their secret place.

The twins would play hide-n-seek beneath the main sanctuary of the church that was centered directly under the pulpit. They could hear the entire

Gambling

sermon, but could only visualize the actual motion. The sound of the choir's movements and the sound of the pastor's voice was as if they were in the same room.

Sometimes they would stop playing and just listen. They knew everyone's voice. It was like a blind person who mastered the sound of footsteps and tones. They would play a game of putting the name to a voice. They often wish they could run upstairs and see if the person they thought was speaking was the correct individual.

The room under the pulpit, their special room, undressed appeared to be larger than it actually was fully furnished. Before the church was remodeled, the room served as a dressing room for the choir. As the church grew, the tiny room became obsolete. After the remodeling of the church, the choir's new dressing room moved to the east wing, leaving the "secret place" unoccupied. The parishioners of the congregation seldom visited the room that had no windows with only one way in and out. When the services were over, they would quietly slip back into the room with the other children and awake Mrs. Jones. Her snorting sounds were as if she was rebuking the devil.

Chapter 3

PEOPLE THAT HAVE LOST THEIR WAY

Once a month after church services, Helen would take the girls to skid row, where they would do missionary work. They would volunteer their services, minister and serve food to the less fortunate men, women and children. Many were well-educated people that, for some reason or other, had lost their way.

During one of their trips, they met a woman name Kathy and her daughter JoAnn. The pale chubby girl, with big eyes and funny looking legs, was the same age as the twins. To Amber and Autumn everyone was equal. They felt no shame in playing with JoAnn, even though her hand-me-down clothing was torn and tattered.

Gambling

Kathy was a victim of domestic violence. Her abuse contributed to her drug addiction. Trying to fill the hole in her soul, she kept sinking deeper into drugs. Penniless and homeless, Kathy and her daughter JoAnn found shelter in a downtown mission. The child, too young to truly understand the dynamics of being homeless, could only dream about the reality of a stable environment.

The church took up a special collection every third Sunday of the month to assure the children who lived in poverty-stricken environments would receive a special gift on Christmas. On Christmas Eve, the missionaries would assist in feeding the hungry. Christmas day, each missionary would adopt a family for the day. It was no surprise when Autumn's family of three chose to adopt Kathy's family of two.

For Christmas, the girls gave JoAnn a kaleidoscope. The optical toy consisted of a cylinder with mirrors and colored shapes inside that create shifting symmetrical patterns when the end was rotated. The young girl had never seen an instrument that had so much beauty in such a small box. GG was very instrumental in helping Kathy find gainful employment, thus allowing her to move to a government subsidized apartment complex while, at the same time, allowing JoAnn to grow up in a nourishing and stable environment.

Chapter 4

LOVE AT FIRST SIGHT

Kathy was unloading her car, at the washhouse, when a man came out from the Laundromat and offered to help her carry her load of laundry. The laundry room, located in the building of the projects, was always busy. Kathy found it more convenient to use the Laundromat across the street from the projects and next to the senior citizen apartment complex.

The man, definitely fifteen years her senior, seemed very respectful and courteous. They exchanged numbers and Joseph started picking Kathy up every Monday so they could chitchat while they did their laundry together.

This friendship quickly grew into love. This relationship was a far cry from the first abusive marriage she suffered with JoAnn's father. That marriage left

Gambling

her and her child penniless and homeless. After exhausting every avenue of survival, they were left with no choice but to live on the streets of skid row. After a year of being clean and dating Joseph, they married in a simple ceremony, with her best friend Sara by her side. They purchased a beautiful home for their new family.

Joseph and Kathy desperately wanted to have a child. Kathy's life was almost complete with Joseph. In her third month of pregnancy, Kathy felt so good she woke up fixed her a bite to eat and went outside into the garden. The birds were in the background singing. She felt so good she began to pick fresh flowers from the garden and a few peaches from the peach tree. As she sang along with the birds, she started to feel a little tired. She sung herself to sleep swinging on the swing in the garden.

She awoke a few hours later and decided to fix a meal fit for a king. She was humming and preparing dinner, short ribs of beef, candied yams, fresh collard greens, dressing from scratch, corn muffins, corn on the cob, and for dessert fresh homemade peach cobbler.

Kathy's only challenge in this relationship was she was never able to conceive a child with Joseph. Later that evening Joseph rushed Kathy to the hospital, where she had a miscarriage. After two miscarriages the doctor told her it was detrimental to her health to try and conceive.

Joseph decided in the best interest of her health, he would have a vasectomy. This was a mutual agreement, but Kathy felt less than a woman not to be able to have a child for the man she loved.

Joseph would call during his lunch hour just to hear her voice. For no special reason, he would pick a few roses from the rose garden, run her bath and fill the tub with rose petals. He always had a plan, when she was feeling down. One time, he called her and told her to be ready in an hour—they were going out to dinner. He failed to tell her they were flying to San Francisco.

The view from their suite overlooked the marina. After dinner they attended a play. On another surprise outing, Joseph had his wife to pack a small overnight bag. They jumped in their SUV, and hours later they arrived in Lake Tahoe.

Kathy was the most important person in her husband's life. Joseph's love was so strong for Kathy that he pampered her in special ways, every day of his life. Joseph was a very successful stockbroker who could afford to spoil his new wife; he knew the value of money and money management.

Chapter 5

All Grown Up

As years passed, the girls in their last month of high school looked forward to graduation. Autumn and Amber graduated with honors. With high grade point averages, they received scholarships that were well deserved. From the time they started talking; GG would faithfully read to them or teach them a new word every night. Although they chose a college away from home, they were reluctant about leaving GG, but she encouraged the girls to pursue their education and attend the college of their choice.

JoAnn was also looking forward to graduation. She knew what was needed to pursue her goals. She recalled the night she and her mother walked the streets with funny and strange looking people that talk to themselves and walked beside them. Some of the people had mismatched shoes and wore layers of clothing in the dead heat of summer. She remembered how tightly her mother held her right hand allowing her left hand free to suck her thumb for comfort and security. As they walked the streets of skid row, seeking shelter, the only thing that stuck in the small child's mind was something an old lady rambled, as she walked beside them. The woman said, "There are two men you should always know, one that has a dollar and one that can get a prayer to God" Although she was a little girl, she never forgot the lady's words. That could have been one of the reasons JoAnn was so adamant about having her own, and never again having to beg for food or sleep on throw away rugs in alleys and feel dirty for the lack of being able to take a bath or brush her teeth.

Looking back on the former years, JoAnn was so grateful that Ms. Helen had been a part of her life. She felt all of her accomplishments would only be a dream, if Ms. Helen had not been such a great role model. Ms. Helen taught JoAnn morals, integrity, and spiritual values.

Growing up in the projects was no challenge to living on skid row. It only served as a rewarding experience. JoAnn always expressed how the acquired skills and observations were tools that enhanced her knowledge in dealing with life's trials and tribulations.

Gambling

While JoAnn was in her last year of high school, she accepted a job as a waitress in a very upscale supper club. After graduation, she was promoted to head host at the Supper Club. Not only did it increase her finances, it left room open for future promotions.

Chapter 6

Look Before you Leap

Amber had ambivalent feelings about leaving Autumn at school and, at the same time, she missed her great grandmother and Tony—the love of her life. Her heart told her she could not go another day living apart from her childhood sweetheart. Her grade point average had dropped. She did not like attending college so far away from home. After her third year in college, she decided she and Tony would get married as soon as possible. Therefore, it was no surprise when they were married in a very small and simple ceremony. Amber had no apparent reason for rushing into her marriage except for love; GG had anticipated giving both the girls an extravagant wedding. Because of final exams, Autumn could not attend her sister's wedding. The happy couple vowed to renew their vows with family and friends in attendance at a later date.

After working a short period, during their first year of marriage, Amber's career in special education was cut short—she was pregnant. Tony felt his income, as a marketing manager, was sufficient enough that his wife did not have to work. He insisted that she resign. Tony looked forward to coming home to a home-cooked meal and sharing the evening with his pregnant wife. Amber was a great cook. A trait she had picked up from GG. Although Amber loved her job working with special needs children, she also respected her husband's wishes.

Tony had four very close friends—Romero, Tom, Floyd and James—all of whom had different occupations, dreams and goals, but they all shared one common interest, which was gambling. On the last Friday of each month, the five friends would take turns hosting a poker game. One Friday, somewhat bored after their traditional poker game, Tom suggested they try their luck at the casino.

The group of five considered the event one of fun and pleasure, never realizing the power of addiction. At first, the games seemed harmless. It did not take long before they discovered the meaning of gambling. As time progressed, Tom, the psychology major of the group, concluded there were three types of gamblers: a winner, a player and a hustler. Tom noticed how the person that called his- or herself the gambler played the game to win. The gambler knew money management and self-discipline, he set limits on the amount he intended to win or lose, he did not loan and he did not borrow to continue gambling. It seemed the gambler's strategy was, to never give a sucker a stick to beat you with. A gambler will squeeze a dollar until it hollers. Their one and only purpose for gambling is to win your money.

On the other hand, you have the player who plays the game to play, with no method or direction. To him, the hundred-dollar chips have no true value, until he goes home a loser. They continued to play, only to slip deeper into debt. Their main objective is to get back the money they lost. They allow the addiction to take over, before they realize the problem exists. Lastly, he concludes that hustlers are individuals that stand around waiting for prey; sit or stand at a poker table day after day, sometimes playing in pairs, and wait for the weakest link. These hustlers have no mercy on their prey.

Usually, hustlers are very talkative, only to divert their victim's attention away from the game.

Chapter 7
A Breath of Fresh Air

The summer crept in without warning, bringing with it a breath of fresh air named Karyn. The baby was cute and cuddly, with rosy cheeks and a smile that would mend a broken heart. Amber spent a lot of time with the baby, taking her to the park and visiting GG. The older the baby got, the more she smothered the child. Losing her parents and grandparents at such a young age, caused Amber to question at times, if maybe she was overly protective.

The autumn leaves, which revealed the amber gloom of fall, were welcome by many. The season caught Tony somewhat off guard. He thought time would bring about a change in Amber's over protection of Karyn. He started to feel neglected, as Amber's weight steadily increased and her confidence slowly declined.

Tony was constantly complaining about Amber's weight. He had become verbally abusive. To make matters worse, during his frequent visits to the casino, instead of his usual glass of wine, he now enjoyed double shots of hard liquor. His repeated gambling losses, his abuse, and their financial matters were growing out of control, and were contributing factors to their declining marriage. Tony, on many occasions, had late meetings that lasted throughout the night. When he finally arrived home, he was always tired, often climbing into bed without dinner. He never took a shower and turned his face toward the wall.

Amber was having a hard time losing the baby fat. With every pound she tried to lose, she would gain two pounds. The constant rejection was an underlying factor to her impulsive eating. No matter what she did, she could not lose the baby fat. Amber was at her lowest point in life. Her marriage was on the rocks and her husband told her she looked like a slob. She knew things had gotten bad; the worse the situation got the more she ate. Amber, disappointed with herself for gaining so much weight, started to accept the blame for Tony's social, psychological and emotional abuse. She kept telling herself that maybe if she could have been in better control of her weight, given her husband more attention and consideration, their marriage may have turned out differently.

Chapter 8

NEVER FORGET YOUR ROOTS

GG was getting older, and not getting around as well as she had in the past. JoAnn had stopped by to bring Ms. Helen's vitamins she had purchased at the health food store. The clerk assured JoAnn the vitamins were good for arthritis.

JoAnn was in shock when Amber walked out of the bedroom in her pajamas, carrying her six-month-old baby on her hips. JoAnn was unaware that Amber and Tony had filed for a divorce and Amber had moved back with GG. Amber had come back to the place she always cherished, into her old bedroom, the house that shared so many childhood memories and the only place she ever called home.

JoAnn recalled the great time they had growing up. Never truly understanding as a kid how dysfunc-

Gambling

tional her life really was, living from mission to mission on skid row, wondering where she and her mother would get their next meal. Often, GG would invite her and her mother over for Sunday dinner. They would sit around the dinner table laughing, talking, and discussing different topics of interest.

JoAnn did not really comprehend the true value and importance of those conversations until now. She was still in disbelief, but grateful that Amber and her baby now lived in the place they could always call home.

As a kid, JoAnn was a chubby little girl, with yellow buckteeth who sucked her thumb. Her eyes were big and round as the earth, and her bowlegs brought more attention to her pigeon toes.

Amber felt even more self-conscious as she noticed the changes in her childhood friend's appearance. JoAnn, a perfect ten, had the look of wealth and sophistication. Her beautiful straight teeth sparkled, like the rock on her baby finger. She lived in a very prestigious neighborhood, owned a plush condominium, and purchased a Lexus straight off the showroom floor

GG never really knew exactly what JoAnn did; she knew she worked in an upscale supper club. However, GG never questioned JoAnn. She accepted her for the person she portrayed, and for the kindness and affection she bestowed on her.

Amber thinking back to her friend's humble beginnings was happy for JoAnn, She looked wonderful. It was obvious life must have been awesome. JoAnn had made a previous commitment, therefore cutting her visit short. She told Amber she would give her a call, and maybe this weekend they could get together for dinner.

Chapter 9

GAMBLING IS LONGER THAN LIFE

After JoAnn graduated from high school, she had saved enough money to lease a condo with option to buy. Joseph and Kathy didn't want JoAnn to move, but she felt her mother, now approaching forty, was entitled to the comfortable life that Joseph provided.

Beside Kathy, Joseph's only other weakness was the stock market. It had been good to Joseph; he had made some wise investments. After years of hard work and some very good investments, the stock market started to decline.

Kathy never doubted Joseph's judgment when it came to financial matters. The day he asked Kathy to sign the papers to refinance the house, she did it without question.

The year the stock market crashed, his spirit was at a loss. He was accustomed to spoiling Kathy. The fact that he could no longer afford the lifestyle that he felt Kathy deserved weakened his heart. Sadly, he had become his own best customer.

He never told Kathy how much money they had lost. He tried to keep her in the lifestyle he had bestowed on her; he never missed giving her a weekly allowance. Hiding the fact he was losing thousands of dollars a day.

To recoup his losses, Joseph borrowed money on his life insurance policy only to invest with no avail. He lost everything they had set aside for a rainy day. As was his custom, every evening he would go to the computer and check the stocks.

Realizing everything was gone; Joseph's heart was heavy and his spirit torn. As he gasped his last breath and slumped over his desk, suffering a massive heart attack.

Before Joseph's death, he was an active member in the Church. Joseph and Kathy seldom missed a service, Joseph sang in the choir and Kathy was an usher. They never missed a Sunday without paying their tithes, and giving their offering.

Without a doubt, Kathy knew that Joseph had prepared for the hereafter. The couple kept their important papers at the bank, in a safe deposit box.

Gambling

Although Kathy never wrote a check or paid a bill, she was knowledgeable where everything was kept.

The next morning after Joseph's death, Sara accompanied Kathy to the bank so they could prepare for her husband's funeral. The shock showed on her face when she opened the safe deposit box and realized there was only a few thousand dollars in the bank account. She was even more shocked when she opened the envelope that contained the life insurance policy and there was a letter that read "I have come to the end of the line financially; I have no bank account, no stocks, and no bonds. The only support I can offer is spiritual. It is up to you and God now. There is nothing too difficult for you and God to handle. You both are winners".

Kathy sat for a while in shock; Sara never said a word. Kathy knew he had died of a broken and stressed heart. He had kept this deep secret, something they never did. They always shared. She was wise enough to know Joseph was a good man.

After a while, she began to cry her tears turning into laughter, realizing that she also had a secret. Thinking how she would drive to the local casino seven miles from home for a few hours, five days a week, between Joseph's lunch hour and the time it took him to drive home. She would lose her weekly allowance every week, leaving her penniless.

Sara still sat silently. Kathy uttered, my Joseph never complained, he was a blessed man. Kathy sent Joseph to heaven in a very special way. Someone sang, while a very thin girl did a praise dance to the tune of "The Battle Is Not Yours, It's The Lord's". The pastor did the eulogy on how God brought dry bones to life. The service ended as they lifted his body into a carriage that was drawn by six white horses. A parade of friends marched behind the casket as the choir sang. They released twelve white doves.

Chapter 10

On My Own Now!

Since the death of her husband, loneliness and despair had become her constant companion. Living alone on a fixed income in a tiny one-bedroom senior citizen complex, struggling to pay medical expenses and, at the same time, trying to fill the hole in her soul; Kathy's health began to fail and she suffered a stroke and many other health problems began to arise. The day the doctor told Kathy that she had diabetes and congestive heart disease, Sara, Kathy's best friend, was there to hold her hand, give her words of encouragement and to assure her that she cared. Kathy's conditions caused her to need the assistance of a wheel chair from time to time.

JoAnn spent the good part of the day preparing for her mother's bus trip. The widow women take the casino bus at least four times a week to the Indian Reservation. Every person that boarded the casino express had a player's card. This card allowed the players to receive a ten dollar cash voucher plus a free meal ticket. The Casino Express fulfills a need. It is a meeting place for senior citizens. Most of which experience the same emotions and the same loss. They look forward to seeing each other. This circle of friends is like a gambling support group. If one person won, they gave 10% of the jackpot to the other members in their circle.

Kathy was the last person to board the Casino Express. As usual, the bus driver helped load her wheelchair and two oxygen tanks. Once boarded and sitting in her regular seat next to Sara, Kathy dosed off reminiscing about her late husband.

Today was exactly two years to the day that her husband died. After the death of Joseph, Sara would drive Kathy to her doctor's appointments and occasionally go to the movies.

After several games of bingo, Sara hit the jackpot. She gave Kathy $500 and loaned her $500. By the time the bus was ready to leave; Kathy was losing and did not want to leave. Sara stayed with Kathy and decided to take the red eye express back that evening. Sara sent her money home by another member of the circle so she would not be tempted to play her winnings and lose. She only kept $200 to

Gambling

play the slot machine. One of Kathy's oxygen tanks was equipped with an energy-conserving device, allowing the tank to last a longer period of time.

The evening bus came and left. They were winning and still did not want to leave. Kathy said she felt better than she had in a long time. Thinking it was her husband's spirit looking over her. By sunrise, they were both broke. Kathy lying on the bench gasping for air, her oxygen tank was depleted. Sara and others were standing over her waiting for the paramedics to arrive. Kathy stayed in the hospital for four days. On the fifth day, Kathy was once again boarding the Casino Express. On the thirteenth day, they were attending her funeral.

Chapter 11

Heartbreak

Days before the funeral, JoAnn rambled through her mother belongings, searching for an insurance policy. Tired and getting nowhere, she decided she would write a check to pay for her mother's funeral and look for the policy later.

JoAnn's heart was broken after losing her mother and best friend. She had a hard time accepting her mother's death. They had planned for everything in life, except death. Kathy told her daughter; Joseph had made a bad decision in the stock market causing them to lose all of their investments. Kathy never told her daughter he borrowed money on his life insurance policy leaving a zero balance. The truth was that Kathy also borrowed money on her policy to cover Joseph's extravagant funeral services, her gambling loses, and her payday loan accounts. Ms. Helen had taught JoAnn and the twins, if you have three dollars, you spend two and you save one. Unlike her stepfather, at the first sign of the stock market's decline, JoAnn withdrew her investment that superseded her losses.

Several days later, knowing this was a day she had dreaded, she faced the awful task of going through her mother's belongings. Struggling with the emotions of the past and looking at the pictures on the walls brought back many memories, as she packed every item piece by piece. The neatly packed boxes reflected the beginning and the end of a life's journey.

It was near dawn. JoAnn was almost finished, with the exception of the small chest with four drawers.

She pulled out the bottom draw that contained color coordinated, neatly folded panties and bras. Underneath the underwear were two small boxes. One box contained old and the other most recent checkbooks. As she read in shock, she couldn't believe her eyes. Most of the canceled checks were payable to the casino.

She wondered why she never realized all signs of her mother's addiction.

JoAnn thought the trips to the casino, with her best friend Sara and their other circle of friends, was all in fun. The monthly allowance that she gave her mother, plus the pension check that she received from her dead husband, should have covered all of her expenses with money left over. Instead, in her recent checkbook were checks she had written the week before her demise, all payable for and representing gambling losses. JoAnn puzzled, couldn't understand why her mother didn't confide in her. She cried so hard she had to use her asthma inhaler, remembering as a kid how Kathy was always there to calm her when her asthma flared up. The thought of her mother's death upset her more.

Chapter 12

THE BEGINNING AND END

Months later, JoAnn, still feeling the stress of her mother's death, called to see if Amber would like to have dinner with her that evening. Amber in the dumps, unemployed, homeless so to speak, and in a dysfunctional marriage, had agreed, but within a split second had changed her mind about dinner. JoAnn assured her they both could use a stress-free night. If it were not for the baby or GG, Amber probably would not get out of bed.

Amber was very hesitant when it came to expressing her feelings. She always considered the emotional response she would have on the other person's life. Somewhat still indecisive, she accepted Amber's invitation.

Amber wondered what JoAnn did for a living. She had not seen or kept in touch with her friend the way she should have, but was grateful that JoAnn had checked on GG, while she and her sister were away at college. The girls had always been close. As much as JoAnn appreciated their friendship, she wondered if Amber could accept her lifestyle

After what seemed like an hour, they arrived at a supper club, right in the heart of the upscale part of town. Instead of JoAnn entering through the front door, she drove around the building to the back entrance. Amber was somewhat puzzled and confused as to why they entered thru the back entrance. This was JoAnn's first visit to the Supper Club, since her mother's death. Once inside, JoAnn was greeted with the utmost love and respect. Everyone whom she passed in the club acknowledged her presence.

A tall slim very attractive man, who was dressed in all white from head to toe, seated them directly in front of the stage before the show started. JoAnn ordered a drink. Amber, really not a drinker, replied to the waiter she would have the same, without really knowing what she had ordered.

The first performer was a comedian; he was very funny and delightful. His jokes were fresh and raw. The next performer sang a beautiful ballad. Towards the middle of the song, the music changed to a different beat, the performer then proceeds to disrobe. In total shock, Amber, shy and embarrassed, was lost for words. She knew how GG had raised her and her sister, although she was of age; she had never seen such a performance. JoAnn at a loss for words noticed the frown on Amber's face, but was not sure which way to interpret her expression.

Chapter 13

Where are the Jobs

Months later, Amber had an interview at the unemployment office. She was having a hard time finding a job that complemented her degree. She was told that she was over-qualified or not qualified for the positions they had available. Feeling her potential for landing a job in her field was very scarce, due to the State's job cuts, she was at a point where she would take just about anything.

During her interview, she received a text message from JoAnn inviting her to a party that evening. She told her she would tell her who, what, and where later. Amber was somewhat indecisive, since the last outing with JoAnn turned out to be like nothing she ever experienced.

Gambling

The evening caught Amber somewhat off guard. People were dancing, laughing, and just having fun. The house of many rooms and beautiful art was a showpiece within itself. As Amber came out of one of the ten bathrooms, she recognized a girl she knew from college named Brenda.

Brenda, not sure which twin she was talking to, was careful not to address Amber by name. After a few minutes of small talk Brenda invited Amber to accompany her to the east wing of the mansion. As they walked past the circular terrace that was surrounded by all sorts of plants, birds of paradise and large beautiful orchids, both ladies could only marvel at the intricate details of the walkway that led to an enormous room where there were more men than women sitting around socializing, drinking and having what seemed to be a good time.

Brenda noticing Amber's apprehension, offered her a small white pill explaining, it would ease her nerves and at the same time suppress her appetite. The thought of a tiny pill to help the weight problem seemed harmless. Brenda was very thin, but shapely with the prettiest hazel eyes that, at times, seemed to change colors with the lighting.

She seemed somewhat eager to introduce Amber to her friends. Amber, lonely for male companionship, had not dated since her breakup with her husband. Although the weight gain made her feel emotionally insecure, she had hopes that with all of her imperfections, new acquaintances would accept her for the person she is inside and not for her outward appearance.

Amber observed a few people passing around what looked like a glass pipe filled with white smoke. Someone passed the pipe to Brenda. She inhaled it with ease. There was no doubt she was not a first time user. Her newfound friend Brenda convinced Amber, a few drinks away from intoxicated, that the key to her slim figure was in the tiny pill that would suppress her hunger.

Still struggling with her insecurities, and not able to find a job, her consistent weight gain was pushing her deeper into depression.

Brenda assured her that she would lose her weight in no time. Unbeknown to Amber, the rush she experienced from the pill she consumed was just the beginning of the end

Chapter 14

HISTORY REPEATS ITSELF

On one of her trips to the unemployment office, Amber was sitting next to a young woman that looked familiar. It was Jade the singer/stripper from the Supper Club. Although Jade did not physically see it, or believe it, the manager told her business had declined leaving him no choice, but to reduce her performances to two nights a month. She recalled a few years back, when people would come from all over the city just to see her performance.

Jade's appearance seemed somewhat altered from their first meeting at the supper club. Her shapely body was now extremely thin, her teeth stained and somewhat rotten from decay, and her acne looked as if the pimples would pop at any given moment. Amber wondered whether it was the poor lighting or good makeup that made Jades appearance look so different in sunlight.

As Amber walked out of the employment office, she noticed a white Mercedes with the hood propped up. Coming from the rear pipe was white smoke that formed perfect lines in the sky. The woman behind the wheel kept turning the key, to no avail.

It looked and sounded as if it was in need of a major tune up, repairs and bodywork. The woman arose from the car in disbelief; Amber realized it was her new acquaintance Jade. Amber offered her a ride. Although she was somewhat embarrassed, she was quick to accept. In the same breath, she explained that, because of her job displacement, she could not afford the up keep of her car. As soon as she fixed one problem, another would accrue. Jade said it would be great if she could drop her off at a friend's house.

In no time, they pulled up in a circular driveway. The trees on both sides of the street dipped in the middle of the Blvd. as if shaking hands to say, "Hi". As the person came closer, Amber realized it was Brenda. Amber had not seen her old college acquaintance since the night of the party. As they shared the small details of that night, it was obvious Amber wanted more drugs, but did not know how to approach her newfound friends.

Brenda invited Amber to stay and hang out with her and Jade. As they sat around listening to jazz,

Gambling

Amber was popping pills while the other two passed the pipe from one to the other. They never stopped to consider the consequences. Amber honestly believed she had found the answer to her weight problem.

Chapter 15

A Sad But Special Day

Autumn graduated summa cum laude—something she had worked hard to accomplish. The only part of her life that was incomplete was not having her identical twin standing next to her on such a special occasion. When the girls were young, they looked so much alike that you could not tell them apart unless they were side by side. They were inseparable; the twins did everything together.

Autumn wished life had turned out differently. It broke her heart to see Amber jobless, with a child, and a broken marriage. Autumn, a certified public account, had all the intentions of pursuing her career. However, she felt it was best that she stayed closer to home, considering GG's failing health and age.

Amber suggested that Autumn move back home with her, GG and little Karyn. The place they always called home. Autumn noticed Amber's tremendous weight gain, but she never made a comment. Realizing her sister's depression and knowing GG was getting older, Autumn thought maybe it would be like the good old times living under the same roof again with GG, little Karyn and her twin sister. She also realized since living on her own in college she loved the privacy of living by herself.

The baby was playing in her playpen, and GG was reading the newspaper. Autumn thought it would be a good time for the sisters to spend some time together, sharing their secrets, riding their bicycles through the parks, shopping or just hanging out.

When the girls started college, GG insisted because they lived so far from home they should have their own individual discount membership cards from Members Only. Amber thought about the fun they had as kids on Saturdays—going from vendor to vendor, sampling all of the tasty snacks in the enormous store that carried every item you could possibly think of plus more.

She liked the idea of getting away for a while. After all, Karyn had grown so fast she needed new clothing. Amber suggested they drive to the discount store since they carried everything, food, clothing furniture and her hidden agenda, snacks. Once inside the large store, the first person Amber noticed was a woman behind a stand handing out samples of different types of chocolate-coated candy. The closer she got to the stand she realized they were the lollipops that Autumn loved so much. It was national candy month. Vendors from all over the world brought different kinds of sweets. Everywhere you looked, you saw vendors representing their State or Nation.

The store was about to close. Time went by so fast they did not realize they had been shopping for hours. Autumn, aware of her sister's financial situation, would not allow her to pay for any of the items in the shopping cart. Knowing her sister's only income was the child support that Tony paid faithfully, she did not mind helping whenever she could. She was glad to buy her niece and sister whatever they needed. Autumn had maintained a steady job and saved her money while attending college. Amber had purchased very few, since her weight gain. Although her weight was coming down, there was no mistaking one twin for the other.

Chapter 16

Yap—Yap

One day, while leaving the gym feeling somewhat depressed, thinking about her twins weight gain, Autumn felt helpless. She had invited Amber to join her as she rode her bike several miles to the gym where they both had membership. These days Amber very seldom took off her pajamas unless she was going to church or running an errand for GG.

Autumn took the short cut through the park. Realizing she was being followed, she peddled faster. The four-legged little thing resembled a dingy white ball of fur. It kept running and yapping behind her bike. The faster she peddled the faster he ran. Autumn finally stopped, scared that when she crossed the intersection he may have been hit by the passing cars. Autumn, softhearted, picked the smelly little creature up and placed the cute, but dirty, dog in her knapsack. He was perfectly content sleeping on her sweaty gym clothes.

Autumn finally arrived home. As she eased the door open, not sure if she could keep the dog, she hoped Karyn was taking her nap. But instead, Karyn was playing in the backyard. When she heard the yapping sounds of the mutt, she ran as fast as she could. Totally out of breath, she embraced the little dog that was almost as small as her.

Autumn waited a few days, before going to the animal shelter, to see if anyone had reported a lost dog, or if he had an identifying chip. Happy and sad at the same time, the fuzzy ball of fur had no chip and there was no report of a lost dog. While at the shelter to be on the safe side, Autumn had the veterinarian to administer the dog all of his shots.

The last stop before heading home was the doggie salon. The doggie looked as if he hadn't had a bath in months. The groomer asked the dog's name and she replied, "Ah, Tramp," never really considering a name before now. When Amber returned to pick up the dog, she didn't recognize him. He was so handsome; he looked like a little white ball of fur with a black bow tie that accentuated his black eyes.

Karyn loved to play with Tramp. She secretly shared her snacks, dinner, and toys with her playmate. Whenever Autumn jingled her keys, Tramp would lay on his back begging her to pick him up, indicating he wanted her to take him for a ride in her knapsack. She eventually brought him a little cart that connected to the back of her bike. He thought he was in doggie heaven. Tramp was a cute little puppy, riding in his little house with his blue jogging suit identical to Autumn's with the exception of the colors. Her suit was pink.

Chapter 17:

Fulfilling a Dream

One evening on her way to GG's house, as she passed the church, she noticed a storefront building for rent with option to buy. The building had living quarters on top and was located between GG's house and the church. She thought this would be a perfect location to open her practice.

The building was large on the inside, with two bathrooms—one upstairs and one downstairs. The three large rooms, with a small kitchen, were perfect for one person just starting to keep house. The downstairs was ideal to start a professional business. The price was reasonable and the surroundings were suitable.

Thinking ahead, she knew the rooms upstairs would make a prefect apartment. Eventually, she had intentions of moving into her own place. At the present time, Karyn slept in the room with Amber, but the day was soon approaching that she would need her own room.

Autumn had received a scholarship, while attending college.

She also worked full-time, dealing with financial matters and preparing taxes. She lived a leisure life while away at college. GG had always instilled the importance of saving for a rainy day. The owner of the storefront was more interested in selling than renting. With a little help from GG, she purchased the building. GG always thought investing in real estate was a wise investment. The owner was so glad to sell for cash, without the red tape, he lowered the price.

Amber and Autumn went to the Members Only club to buy the necessities to set up the office building. Jimmy, the handyman who always worked at the church, helped the parishioners with small chores whenever he had the time. He had watched the twins grow from childhood to beautiful women. When Autumn called Jimmy, he was more than happy to lend a helping hand.

The more Autumn thought about the large apartment upstairs, the more she entertained the thought of moving. She was used to living alone from her college days. But she was not sure if GG would understand her leaving the family home.

The family was seated for dinner, when Autumn dropped little hints. She said, "Karyn is growing so fast it is time for Karyn to have her own room." She also mentioned the upstairs of the office would be perfect for her to set up housekeeping, because the first couple of weeks before she opened her practice she would be up all hours of the night going through paperwork and organizing files.

Her plans were to open her practice in a few weeks. Autumn, a very proficient and successful Certified Public Accountant, knew it was only a matter of time before her business would flourish. Autumn asked her sister if she would like to work for her, as her personal assistant. Amber, somewhat reluctant because of her drug use, wondered if she could function on a daily basis. On her last leg financially, looking thin and pale, she had become a product of the environment and people she associated with.

Her downward spiral, paranoia behavior and drug use, mixed with a high dose of depression and inability to cope with small tasks, made her wonder if she was capable of being an assistant. Amber's consistent mood swings and fatigue contributed to her low self-esteem.

Amber took a good look in the mirror, looking at the reflection of the person that she had become. She decided that if her sister had that much faith in her abilities to perform on a daily basis, she would seek help for her addiction.

Autumn thought, if Amber had a secure income, and worked side-by-side with her, she would have a brighter outlook about her life.

Chapter 18

THE CLIENT LIST

The client list was growing so fast that Autumn had to hire another accountant to pick up some of the slack. Shawn, the new accountant, with a very impressive resume and still attending school, was more than eager to work with Autumn. The twin had a reputation for being one of the best Certified Public Accountants in the field.

The girls were putting away files, and clearing off their desk. It had been such a hectic week everyone in the office was looking forward to the weekend. It was around closing, when a well-dressed man in his late twenties walked into the office—seeking financial advice. It was not hard for Autumn to greet the well-groomed young man. The pleasant smile on her face told the whole story. After a few deep breaths,

Gambling

she asked, "How can I assist you?" As he blushed, he said, "My name is Kevin Michaels, I am the C.E.O. of a computer software company. I have three other partners. We started our own business, and we are in need of an accountant." Autumn looked at the clock. It was 15 minutes before closing, but she was used to long hours. She told her two assistants to go home, she would be happy to take care of Mr. Michaels. Autumn spent lot of time with Kevin auditing his books that were unacceptable to the IRS. The firm that handled his account before had cost his company a large penalty.

One evening after the two had worked all day on his audit, Kevin asked Autumn out to dinner. Autumn did not hesitate in accepting the invitation. After all, she was smitten by his good looks, poise, self-confidence, and his mannerism. He never allowed her to open a door, or sit in a chair without his assistance. He was the perfect gentleman.

The Supper Club, which consists of a hotel and casino, was a well-deserved outing. It was a welcome sight with the sculptured ceilings that would adorn a queen, and the glass elevators that gave you a view of God's heavenly earth.

Autumn, because of her busy schedule, had not had a date in quite some time. The waiter brought her the menu. Everything looked so good, and it reminded her of when she was a kid, going to the Members

Only store with GG. It was like letting a kid loose in a candy store and saying, "You can have whatever you want." All she ever wanted was a lollipop.

After dinner, Kevin suggested that they go upstairs to the lounge and have a drink and listen to the people sing karaoke. Autumn was a great singer herself, so she loved the idea. Remembering the day when GG made the decision to hire the girls a voice teacher was one of the happiness days of the twins' life.

Kevin was shocked when Autumn decided to sing. When she got on the stage, she brought down the house. Kevin had no idea she had a voice like a bird. After her performance, that was all he talked about. He was totally blown away, by her beautiful voice.

Chapter 19

THE UPS AND DOWNS OF BUSINESS

As the weeks passed, they spent a lot of time at the club. Because of the declining economy, it was somewhat of an off month for her accounting business. Some of her clients lost major accounts. Amber now quite confident in her position, Autumn felt that if necessary, she and Amber could handle the business by themselves.

One night as they entered the club the manager approached Autumn with a job offer as the Master of Ceremony. She was very apprehensive, but accepted, since she was only going to work three nights a week. Besides, the money would subsidize her income, allow her to keep both assistants, and spend more time with Kevin.

Everyone that sang thought they were the best. With Autumn's new job came many new acquaintances. People took for granted that Autumn had some kind of influence with the music industry since she was the M.C. three nights a week. Although she never considered a career as a singer, she had one of the most beautiful voices one has ever heard.

Missy, a regular that frequented the club, almost every night, while waiting to be discovered as a singer, worked as a manager for a Pay-A-Day loan company. She received a percentage for every new customer that took out a loan. When she was not singing, she was in the casino looking for a loser that needed a quick loan. Missy had no kids, no family to speak of and no steady boyfriend.

She loved the thought of being in the lime light, singing every night for free, but at the same time she was pushing her profession as a legalized loan shark. Her clients never saw her true character. People described Missy as that singer that always wore an orchid in her hair, a sweet, soft spoken, compassionate woman that would bend over backward to try to help her clients get a loan. Her entire mannerism was all a facade.

Chapter 20:

Loan Shark

There were as many Pay-A-Day loan companies as liquor stores, and as many losers as churches. Missy knew she had the advantage over the other Pay-A-Day loan companies, because her employer was located directly across the street from the Supper Club

Autumn and Missy had become good friends. After the lounge closed, the women would go downstairs to the casino. One night, as they entered the elevator leading to the casino, a woman approached Missy and asked her was she the LLS? {Legalized Loan Shark} She replied, "Yes." The woman said a friend referred her. She shared the sad story of how she had lost all of her money at the card tables and thought that maybe she could help her in obtaining a loan. She inquired as to exactly how the loan process worked.

Missy explained that you write her company a check for three hundred dollars and they would give you two hundred and fifty five dollars cash and the company would cash your check on your next payday. Missy explained the forty-five dollars is a finance charge, and that the loan is payable payday to payday.

Missy told her at that time, if she still did not have the whole three-hundred dollars for the first loan, she has several friends that work at various Pay-A-Day loan companies in the lower income part of town that would give her a second or third loan to pay the interest on the first.

Autumn somewhat remembered one of her customers (they were discussing the reason they got caught up in this process) said that, according to California State laws, the customer has to pay the face value before the company can advance that person another loan. Therefore, the customer goes from loan shark to loan shark to pay the principal on the loans. She said this is how the customer gets stuck in the loan process. They have to pay the full loan amount before they can redo the loan process.

As Autumn added it in her head, she asked Missy, "If you are paid weekly, borrow two hundred and fifty-five dollars, and pay back three hundred dollars, after three weeks you have paid back one hundred thirty five dollars in so-called finance charges. Is that true? Missy just looked at her with a frown accompanied by a slight smirk, never answering the question.

Chapter 21

Gambling's Payoff

Kevin spent a lot of time at the club sitting at the bar listening to Autumn singing or introducing the next act. If he got bored, while waiting for Autumn to finish her gig at the karaoke club, Kevin would pass time playing cards downstairs at the casino.

The gambling paid off well for Kevin. He was able to pay his IRS debt and helped Autumn with her financial reasonability.

Many nights after work, Autumn would sit behind Kevin studying every hand that he and the other poker players played. At first, she found the game boring, at the same time it looked interesting—not to mention all the money Kevin was winning.

After several weeks of watching and learning, Autumn thought she had mastered the game. She felt with her mathematical skills, and degree in accounting that she had the advantage over the other players. When it came to numbers, she was a math genius.

Thinking she had mastered the game, she decided to try her luck at the poker table. Autumn's downfall was bluffing. Since the losers seldom showed their hand, she never learned the strategy of deception. Many hands looked good to Autumn. She would win one hand and lose three.

One night Kevin decided to sit behind Autumn and watch her play. Kevin, a seasoned player, realized her failures were not only the many hands she played, but also in the method in which she played the hands. Something she never considered was the fact that people bluff and played partners. Later on that night, Kevin explained to her the ins and outs of bluffing, and the fact that some players cheat. This knowledge should have made her a more observing and a tighter player.

Tonight was an off night, at the karaoke bar. Everyone wanted to watch the big Texas Hold'Em tournament that was located downstairs in the casino. Autumn had never seen a real live tournament. Many celebrities participated in this prestigious feature televised event. A quick learner, Autumn picked up many tips by watching the professionals at their best game.

Chapter 22:

Granny's Pain

The rainy weather did not help Ms. Helen. Her arthritis was taking its toll. The cramps in her legs crept up at unexpected hours of the morning. Amber was the one at GG's side, applying hot towels and hand massages to her legs, trying to alleviate the pain. One morning, after Amber had rubbed down GG's legs, GG inquired as to Autumn's whereabouts. "After all," GG said to Amber without thinking, "Baby its 5:00 in the morning, nothing open this time of the morning but legs." Amber smirked, thinking to herself legs and casinos.

The twins, approaching their twenty-fourth birthday, helped GG with chores around the house, took her to doctor's appointments, grocery shopping, and all church functions. GG's failing health was a

Gambling

negative for her, but turned out to be a positive for Amber.

When Amber drove GG to her church functions, she always stayed for the full service. Subconsciously Amber knew this was a well thought plan that GG had schemed up. It served as a reminder of her religious upbringing.

The therapy classes that Amber attended twice weekly played a big part in her drug recovery. Although she had come a long way, she still wasn't out of the woods. The twelve-step program taught her to take one step at a time. It brought her back to the higher power that she had forgotten, while she innocently got caught up in the moment, trying to lose the weight, please her now ex-husband and fill the void in her soul.

Before she knew it, she was caught up in a lifestyle she had never known, caught up in a world she wished never existed.

GG was a big help with Karyn, since she now attended preschool. Autumn made sure her sister's work schedule coincided with Karyn's preschool schedule. Amber would drop Karyn off and pick her up, leaving GG to baby-sit only a few hours a day, while Amber worked and attended drug counseling. GG loved watching Karyn grow up. Karyn was a good baby. She would sleep practically all night. Karyn, a big girl now, was potty trained, drinking out of a plastic cup, putting her toys in her toy box, and could count to ten. She could even recite some of her A-B-Cs.

Autumn thought this would be a good time to plan her move to the upstairs apartment. She called Jimmy to see what his schedule was like for the weekend. The accounting firm was closed Saturday and Sunday and, with the help of Jimmy, they converted the rooms upstairs from the empty cold rooms to a beautiful bachelorette apartment. Autumn had very good taste. She quickly grew out of the person that she once was during college days. When she made a purchase, she bought the best. The furniture was very tasteful; the rugs and window decor were plush. Autumn was eager to show off her latest accomplishments. The next morning, when Amber and Shawn came into the office, they couldn't believe their eyes. The upstairs apartment was fully furnished and decorated in earth tone colors, with matching accessories.

Autumn knew her schedule at the karaoke club and her extra-curricular activities demanded late hours. GG was aware of Autumn's job at the Supper Club, but had no knowledge of the gambling.

GG was sitting in the living room, seemly in good spirits, when Autumn came home early to break the news of her move. Autumn explained she would still spend some nights with her family and some nights at the apartment. GG told her to keep the keys to her house and she was welcome to drop by or spend the night anytime—and it wasn't necessary to call before coming.

In some ways, Amber was glad to once again have her room to herself. Karyn had so many toys; the room she shared with her mother was pretty congested. Karyn, growing so fast, loved her own room. She rode her little car around the house, as Tramp chased behind her, trying to jump so he too could go for a ride.

-

Chapter 23:

First One In

From a distance, the sky was so clear it revealed the beauty of the dissipating snow on the mountaintop. Today was a beautiful day. The Sun was shining bright, the birds were singing, a tall man was edging and trimming the hedge bushes, leaving that fresh smell of cut grass, and the flowers gave off an aroma that could only come from the heavens above.

Amber was always the first person to arrive at the office. After dropping Karyn off at the day care center, she would go directly to work making sure all the accounts were current, filing the flow of paper work, and scheduling future appointments. Tuesday was the day Autumn made her weekly bank deposits.

Gambling

Amber and Shawn were doing such a good job at the office, Amber suggested to Autumn that, since she had the night off at the karaoke club, after she finished her banking business, she should consider taking the rest of the day off and maybe later on that evening, stopping by the house to see Karyn and GG. Autumn thought it was a great idea. She had been working three jobs, so to speak, one at the office, another at the club, and wee hours of the morning at the casino—gambling.

As Autumn entered the bank, a woman was standing at the front door asking every customer their needs and at the same time directing them to their proper destination. The atmosphere was friendly, but the lines were too long. There were empty booths with no tellers. The express line was the longest. It was the first of the month. The bank was crowded as if it were payday for half the population of the city.

The merchant's line seemed even longer. Autumn stood in line for what seemed like an eternity, before deciding to leave. Indecisive as to how she planned to spend her day, she knew in the back of her mind she wanted to return to the casino to try and recouped her losses from last night.

Kevin stayed out late with Autumn, the previous night, knowing he had an early meeting with a new client. He finally convinced Autumn that the casino stayed open 24/7 and that he was tired and she should have been tired also. After all, she was working morning and night.

Autumn knew how to multitask, plus she loved the attention she received from singing and the crowds she drew from gambling with a little schooling from Kevin and watching the pros. She thought she had the game mastered. She felt she was just going through a little losing spree. After all, she thought, "It happens to the best gamblers."

Chapter 24

The Game Kids Play

It was customary that Autumn would valet park, but as she drove into the parking lot she got lucky. A man was pulling out of a parking space just steps front the entrance that led to the poker room. As she entered the casino, she could not help but notice a woman dressed in an all-purple outfit, complemented by a big purple Orchid on the right side of her hair. As their eyes met, Autumn was greeted with a big hug. It was Missy working her business, scouting the casino for losers that needed a quick loan. Mainly the losers that receive a once a month check that had exhausted their funds, and did not have any means of getting money until the first of next month. It was the best bonus time of the month for Missy who never gambled.

Most older players (the regulars) frequented the casino every day, if they had money or not. They knew if one of the regulars hit a jackpot, or if they won, they would spot their buddy until the first of the next month. The older generation always looked out for each other. They thought with their years of experience they could out play the new comers that had no fear. Barely twenty-one, the youngsters thought they knew all the tricks of the trade. They thought gambling was a piece of cake. They had pockets full of money and a lot of slick talk. If they bet a bluffing hand, and no one called, they would proudly show their hands allowing you to see, that if you had called, you would have won. While the youngsters gathered their chips from the table, they would mutter their favorite comment "money never came with instructions." This statement infuriated Autumn to no ends. She knew most of the players at her table, either from the karaoke club or from playing at the same table.

The floor person was eager to seat Autumn; she very seldom had to wait for a seat at a table. She gambled for high steaks always big money games. In appreciation, when she won, she would give the floor person that seated her in what she called her lucky seat, a large tip.

A crowd of people were waiting for seats; therefore, prompting the floor person to start another game.

Gambling

Autumn sat in her favored seat thinking she would be lucky enough to win back the money she lost last night. It did not happen she started losing. Trying so hard to recoup her losses with her last money, she started to bluff. She received several calls; knowing she was bluffing with no chance of winning. She tried to discard her hand without anyone seeing her cards. Before she could mock the hand a player shouted, "I want to see your hand." She knew it was to her disadvantage and their advantage allowing the other players to see her discarded cards. They would have a better idea as to how she played her hand. Kevin neglected to explain when you bluff your facial expressions are of the utmost important. Without a poker face you are doomed before you start. Autumn had a kind sincere honest look. Her eyes kept blinking her hands shaking and her lips had a twitch. Seasonal gamblers could read her facial expressions they knew she was bluffing.

At a player's request, she had no choice but to display her losing hand. Someone in the crowd yelled out, "We have a live fish that doesn't know how to play." That made Autumn more furious. After several more hands she lost all the money she had in her possession. Missy, and other spectators, watched as she scrapped the bottom of her purse for money. Someone suggested that she could go to the cashier's cage and write a check. She thought for a minute then placed one dollar on the table in front of her seat, allowing the dealer to hold her seat for ten minutes.

She had no money except the weekly business deposits that was secured safely in the trunk of her car. As she approached her car she pushed her remote button, but nothing happened. As she pulled the handle to open the door, without hesitation it opened. Looking for the briefcase that contained the weekly deposits frantically, she opened the trunk. There was nothing there. She proceeded to the front of the car. Her heart skipping several beats, sweat beads formed on her nose and upper lip. Looking under the seats, around the side of the doors and in the glove compartment of the car. There was nothing there. Autumn tracked her footsteps back to her beginnings. She remembered entered the parking lot. Rushing to get the parking space, she then realized that she had inadvertently left the car door unlocked.

Chapter 25:

THE REPORT

A security guard noticed Autumn bent over in her car with a flashlight probing for something. He asked if she needed help. She explained that she forgot to lock her car door and someone took the briefcase that contained her business deposits. The security guard flagged down a patrolling police car. A slightly heavy police officer pulled up and made a police report, he called a finger print technician, checked the surveillance camera, and informed Autumn, tomorrow someone would come by her office to get a list of the checks that were stolen. Meanwhile, he told her to make sure her clients were informed of the robbery as soon as possible.

As Autumn entered the back entrance of the casino sucking on her strawberry lollipop, dazed and confused, Missy and the lookie loos (losers) greeted her. Missy was whispering something in her ear, but Autumn was so despondent she did not hear a word.

As Autumn stumbled to the table to retrieve the dollar she had left, she noticed another player sitting in the seat she occupied an hour ago. The chips in front of him were stacked in the shape of a pyramid there were so many she lost count. She stood behind him in disbelief as she watched him win one hand after another, in the same seat in which she had lost hand after hand.

Confused and in total dismay, mentally and physically drained, Autumn drove to GG's, desperately wanting and needing the support of her twin. She tried to comprehend the events of the day. With her lollipop in one hand the steering wheel in the other, Autumn drove into the driveway. The crocodile tears were rolling down her cheeks, the snot covered her top lip and the palms of her hands were damp with sweat. She sat in her car, shaking with apprehension, knowing eventually she would have to face the reality of her actions. Autumn's firm was responsible for the payroll of several small accounts. Not only had she lost her personal money, she had lost the accounting firms money. One of those accounts, Boo's Boutiques, a small clothing store, had hired her firm to prepare their payroll. The boutiques would give Autumn's

Gambling

accounting firm cash money to cover their weekly payroll.

She did not see Amber's car as she eased into the driveway. Suddenly it dawned on her. Tonight was Amber's therapy class. She knew, regardless of the circumstances, without a doubt, she had her sister's unconditional love and support. Amber would stand by her, through thick and thin. Although she knew she could divulge her utmost secrets to her twin, feelings of guilt, embarrassment and shame had begun to run their course.

In total shock and looking desponded, Autumn, totally confused, quietly entered the house and slipped into the bathroom. She washed her face and hands without being noticed. She hoped that GG and Karyn would be in the family room watching television or playing a game. Instead, as Autumn came out of the bathroom down the hall, GG and Karyn met her half way on their way to the kitchen. With those piercing grey eyes, GG took one look at her great-granddaughter and asked, "Baby what's wrong?" Autumn really did not want to burden GG with her problems, but there was no need in trying to avoid the truth. She knew GG could look straight through her. She probably knew already. After all, people always said, GG could see into the future. Autumn still had her key so it was nothing unusual for her to drop by unannounced or spend the night making a bed on the let-out couch.

Autumn could not help but burst into tears as she told her great-grandmother the sad events of the day. Autumn thought back to the day GG realized Amber had harbored a secret. GG did not fuss; she expressed to Amber how much she loved her. She said, "Families had overcome worse obstacles in life. That sometimes God has to take you through to bring you out" GG insisted that Autumn spend the night with the family, get a good night's rest and they would deal with the problems tomorrow.

Autumn called the insurance company with a small shred of hope that maybe, maybe there was a loophole under which she was covered under the policy. The woman on the other end informed Autumn that the insurance policy did not cover negligence; she was responsible for the firm's loss.

Chapter 26:

The News

The neighborhood dogs barked at the paperboy, as Kevin retrieved the morning paper. Sipping on his hot coffee, he almost choked, reading the small column on the front page of the morning newspaper with the heading, "Accountant Loses Clients' Money at Local Casino". He called Autumn's cell phone and, after a few rings, he hung up. Questioning why Autumn had not called, he jumped in his car and drove straight to her office.

With all the commotion, Autumn had totally forgotten to call Kevin. No one noticed as Kevin walked into the office building unannounced. Once inside her office, he understood how she could have forgotten. But he couldn't comprehend how she could be so careless. Her office was in total chaos.

The phones were ringing off the hook. Amber and Shawn were busy examining their files, talking to various banks, calling customers and checking their ledgers. Autumn told Kevin the story at the same time, apologizing to Kevin as if it was his loss instead of hers.

That evening, as Autumn and Kevin entered the club, everyone looked at the couple as if they had the plague. Feeling uncomfortable and irresponsible as they watched the expressions, and seeing the regular players whisper as they walked by, it made her more furious. She wondered how she could MC with the feelings of guilt and stupidity. She hoped one of the regulars or lookie loos may have heard gossip pertaining to her losses, but all they did was speak. Missy was busy soliciting a new client. She told Autumn they would talk later.

Kevin walked around the casino trying to get information, while Autumn went upstairs to inform the manager of the karaoke club she couldn't perform tonight. With all the publicity, surrounding the incident, the manager of the karaoke bar told her he thought it best for business that she resigns. She was in total agreement. After all, she had personal obligations that needed her immediate attention.

The glass elevator seemed as if it took forever to reach the lower level that lead to the casino. At first, she did not see Kevin sitting at the poker table conversing as he folded his losing hand. As she made her way to the table where he was sitting, the floor man stopped her. He expressed his sadness at her misfortune. He said he would keep his eyes and ears open. He knew the amount of money she had lost in the last couple of nights. The fact that she was a large tipper and drew a crowd was all-good for the casinos business.

Autumn walked over to Kevin as he folded another hand. The oh-so-familiar look on Autumn's face, sensing that she wanted to play, Kevin reached in his pocket and gave Autumn five hundred dollars. The floor man quickly found her a seat. As usual, she lost before the seat got warm. The floor man, realizing her dilemma, and knowing she was a high roller, assumed, at the present time, she had excellent credit. He told the dealer to lock up her seat. The dealer precipitated, placing a dollar chip in front of her favorite spot.

The floor man, then in a whisper, suggested that she could go to the cashier's cage and apply for a line of credit. The man in the sky (The people that are paid to watch the activity on the casino floor) advised the casino manager to approve her request. Within minutes, she was approved for a five thousand dollar marker, payable in seven days. On her way back to the table she bumped into Kevin on his way to the men's room. Trying to acquire information regarding Autumns tragedy the previous night, he lost all the money he had won the nights before; therefore, he was ready to leave. Autumn told Kevin she had to pick up her chips and she would meet him in the valet.

Autumn, ashamed to tell Kevin she lost again, separated her money making sure she put the five hundred dollars Kevin had given her, in a separate compartment of her purse. Before leaving she thanked the floor person for putting in a good word to the casino manager, avoiding her from going through the usual check cashing procedures. Embarrassed she told the casino manager she had an emergency and she would see him tomorrow.

Once inside the car Kevin inquired as to how she came out.

She lied feeling guilty she told him she made a few dollars. Thinking it was only right because of his losses she handed him back the five hundred dollar that he had given her.

Chapter 27

ANOTHER DAY'S JOURNEY

JoAnn read about Autumn's travesty. She immediately called Autumn and offered her financial assistance. Since the insurance company would not cover the mishap, it caused Autumn to exhaust most of her personal funds. Purchasing the building, buying new furniture and decorating had been very costly, leaving little money to cover the five figure payroll accounts. With the money JoAnn loaned her, she was able to replace the cash deposits plus hold on to the remaining money from the marker she received from the casino cage.

Thinking different surroundings and unfamiliar faces would change her luck; Autumn drove ninety miles to a casino where she had never been. As she familiarized herself with her surroundings she saw a sign that lead her to the poker room. Several names were on the casino board, which displayed the names of players ahead of her that were waiting for a seat at the poker table.

The difference in this casino and her local casino was she couldn't pay the floor person for a seat; she had to wait her turn. Standing on the sideline, waiting for a seat, she observed two locked seats. Autumn looked at the time knowing they could only hold the seat for ten minutes. She knew she was the fifth person in line for a seat. Twenty minutes had gone by finally they returned. She watched them play a hand and what followed next left Autumn in total disbelief.

Finally the floor person called her name to a different table. Just as she reached the table, a woman with several racks of chips was standing up to leave. The woman gave her a strange stare as the floor man offered Autumn the empty seat. After a few hours the woman came back standing around swallowing bets and trying to start small talk. The more Autumn looked at the woman the more familiar she looked. Autumn thought maybe the women had sung one night at the karaoke club. Shortly after, another lady walked up and started talking. One of the ladies laughed, as the two were deep in conversation. Suddenly it dawned on Autumn. It was Brenda, an acquaintance from school. Brenda introduced the

Gambling

two. Brenda thought how good Autumn looked—tired but otherwise, in good physical shape. Jade, at first, thinking it was Amber, took a double look. Jade somewhat nonchalant, had locked up her seat at the poker table. She had been walking the floors of the casino busy trying to score a date. She desperately needed money to buy food for her two kids that were asleep in her van, before she spotted Brenda standing behind Autumn. The pair stood behind Autumn until she was completely broke.

Chapter 28

IF MONEY ONLY CAME WITH INSTRUCTIONS

Missy did not care who borrowed money from her company or who she referred for a loan, as long as they had the means to pay the money back. Considering Autumn was raised with morals and values, Missy felt she would be the last person to renege on her loan. Missy also had been around long enough to know gambling doesn't discriminate—it has no boundaries. Most people venture into gambling with good intentions, but get caught up in a tangled web of deceit with no way out.

Trying to win the five thousand to buy back her marker from the casino/supper club, she kept telling herself that all she needed was a bankroll. Missy told her she truly understood her predicament and, since she was her friend, she would introduce her to someone that might be able to help. Autumn thinking she sincerely was concerned, agreed to the meeting. Missy made a call; within a few hours a well-dressed man, named Sean, and Missy were sitting in the lounge having what seemed to be a serious conversation. Before the two got up from their seat, he passed Missy a white envelope.

Autumn was down to her last money. As she stood up playing her last hand of black jack, she had a clear view to the lounge. Autumn remembered Sean, the man Missy was talking to, from the casino ninety miles away.

Autumn was standing on the sideline, waiting for a seat. She recalled Jade and the man were playing at the same table. Autumn saw the dealer place a dollar in front of Jade's chair, thus holding her spot for ten minutes. Seconds later, the man locked up his seat. They left for fifteen or twenty minutes. As the man passed the floor person, he slipped him a twenty-five dollar chip, so that the floor person would ignore the time limit of ten minutes.

When Jade returned, she sat back down in the seat she had locked, tossed the dealer the chip and told him, "Deal me in." The man in question, that gave Jade the money, sat back down in his seat at the same table. In a single hand that they were playing heads up, he won back the money he paid her for services rendered.

Autumn made up her mind if this was about prostitution it wasn't even under consideration. She wasn't going to sell her soul to pay a gambling debt. Just as Autumn lost her last hand, Missy and the man were walking toward her.

After the two were introduced, Sean indicated that he would loan her money on her vehicle. He explained to her that he had to put a tracking device on her car. She could keep the car to drive, but he needed the pink slip. She would owe ten percent interest every week. If she missed two payments, he would repossess the car.

Autumn agreed to his terms, her only problem was she didn't have her pink slip. It was locked in her safety deposit box at the bank. Missy, eager to keep the white envelope, told Sean that she would vouch for Autumn. Missy knew Autumn would give him the signed slip in the morning, as soon as she could get to her safe deposit box. Sean said he was breaking his rules. He didn't conduct business in that manner. Missy gave her word. If he gave Autumn the money, she would meet him the first thing in the morning with the pink slip. Autumn borrowed enough money from the stranger to pick up her marker and have enough left over to place another bet. She paid the marker only to rewrite the check.

Gambling

Before the night was over she had lost the extra money she borrowed, and the marker she paid. Totally confused, her mind told her the more money she had the better her chances of winning. Because of the negative publicity, the casino would not accept another marker, but did accept her personal check.

Chapter 29

The Trust

Autumn had no idea what to do. She had four hundred dollars left to her name. She already borrowed money from JoAnn. She had several outstanding Pay-A-Day loans, a five thousand dollar check, and the six thousand dollars—plus interest she borrowed on her car.

As usual she called Missy for help. Missy suggested that Autumn go to the bank an open a line of credit on her office/apartment building. They both thought this was a good idea. That way, Autumn could pay off all of her debts.

The building was free and clear. Autumn and GG had paid cash for the building.

Business had declined since the article appeared in the newspaper. The separate entrance on the side

Gambling

that led to Autumn's apartment upstairs was a blessing. It separated her office from her apartment.

The only way Amber knew if Autumn was at home was whether or not her car was in the driveway. Amber knew if Autumn's car wasn't visible Autumn was not home. The twins hadn't seen much of each other lately. Amber had no idea of her sister's predicament.

When Amber arrived early to the office, Autumn was usually asleep. Amber never knew most mornings Autumn had just come home from a long night of gambling at the casinos.

The firm had suffered a big setback since the article in the newspaper. Amber and Shawn made several calls to no avail, trying to regain the trust of their past clientele. Autumn knew business had declined, but she was so wrapped up in her social life, that it didn't seem to matter.

The morning was going by too fast. She knew how important it was to keep a promise. She had given Sean her word. She promised him she would hand over her pink slip for the money he had given her last night. Feeling irresponsible, foolish and thoughtless, the money was gone nothing had been accomplished. She was facing a worse dilemma than ever.

The loan officer at the bank informed her it would take a few days to process the loan application. In total dismay, she couldn't figure out what to do when suddenly she remembered. Her name was on GG's checking account. Amber and Autumn handled most of GG's personal affairs. Sweating from nervous anxiety she decided to borrow the money out of her great-grandmother's bank account. She knew she could put the money back in a few days when the loan was approved. Autumn was so busy gambling and handling her own business that she was oblivious to what was happening with GG's account.

After GG gave Autumn the money to buy the building she felt it wasn't necessary to bother Autumn with the small details of her finances, so she had Amber to transfer most of her money from her checking and savings into CDs (certificates of deposit). Looking at the clock, it was almost ten. If she drove fast, she could make it to her safe deposit to retrieve her pink slip and drive to GG's bank before noon.

When she checked GG's balance, there was only a couple of thousand dollars in the account. Autumn knew GG had overdraft protection allowing her to write a check for seven thousand dollars leaving her extra money to gamble.

Very nervous, Missy met her at the entrance of the casino hoping and praying that she had the signed pink slip. Sean was a no-nonsense type of guy. He didn't play when it came to his money. She went to the cashier's cage to pick up her personal check, but the lady at the cage informed her that her check was

Gambling

sent to the bank that morning. The bank account the check was drawn on was on the other side of town she thought if she got to the bank the first thing in the morning, when the doors open, she could put the money in her account before the check from the casino was presented for payment.

Missy was waiting patiently while Autumn took care of her business at the casino cage and, at the same time, wondering what was taking so long. Missy was anxious for Autumn to take care of her business with Sean. After all, she was their connection. Sean had given Missy her regular percentage for a finder's fee.

Just as they passed the blackjack tables, headed to the lounge, they saw Sean sitting at a table sipping on a cocktail.

He greeted Autumn with a big smile. She handed over the slip with pride and honor knowing she had kept her word. As she walked across the street to pay off the Pay-A-Day loan, she had with Missy's company, she thought about what GG had always said. "Your word is your bond. Without a word you have no honor." With some of the money she borrowed, she drove to the other side of town to pay off a few of her other outstanding payday loans—already a couple of days past due.

The poker section of the casino, where Autumn was standing, was a dead zone. You couldn't receive incoming calls.

The bank had left several messages telling her that the deed on her building read Helen and Autumn not Helen or Autumn. This meant it was in joint tenancy and she needed her great-grandmother's signature in order to take a loan out on the property. She would never consider asking GG to borrow money on the building. Autumn already owed past due property taxes that GG knew nothing about. With her failing health and frugal lifestyle, it could cause GG's early demise.

Autumn's lifestyle had become a game of chess. Lost for words, she had run out of options. The only person that might have an answer was GG, but there was no way she could tell GG how she had stolen money out of her bank account, and how, for months, she had betrayed her trust.

Shawn was the junior accountant of the firm. She had done her best to keep the business afloat. Amber had learned a lot since teaming up with her sister, but she still had a lot to learn. On the other hand, Shawn knew the firm had seen its hay days, and now it was facing its end.

Today was the first time in months that Autumn had actually come downstairs ready for work at a reasonable hour, but judging from her facial appear-

Gambling

ance, it was bad news. With tears in her eyes, she announced the closing of the firm. Amber and Shawn knew this day was coming. Shawn loved her job and her mentor so much. She would have worked for free. Facing student loans, and other obligations, she had no choice but to seek other employment. Amber felt the pressure of her sister's pain, without knowing the real core of the problem—gambling. Amber thought, since the building was paid for the few accounts they had in the past months would cover the utilities and other trivial expenses. Amber didn't see the whole picture, because she didn't know the whole story.

GG was a little under the weather these days not getting around so well. She wanted so bad, since she didn't give Amber an extravagant wedding, to give the twins a big surprise twenty-sixth birthday party.

Autumn asked her sister not to tell GG about her travesty. Autumn had an unrealistic belief that since GG seldom came by the office she would never know she had closed shop. Her thought pattern had ceased working. These days, Autumn had a gambling crack addiction.

Today, Autumn arrived early at GG's house; she planned on spending the day with her family. Lately she had a motive for every move she made. Autumn stayed over at GG's house, to intercede the mail, hoping the overdraft statement would arrive. She knew the bank probably would send a notice of the overdraft within a couple of days. She wanted to make sure that she was the one to retrieve the mail. Amber and GG were happy to have her home. Karyn played games with her aunt, while Tramp begged to go for a ride. But it seemed somewhat odd for Autumn to spend two nights in a row.

Although GG could see some events before they happened. The stress on Autumn's face was apparent that something was happening. GG never said a word. She was content having her family together sitting around the dinner table listening to fabrications of Autumn's life.

Chapter 30

CLOSING DAY

It was closing day. The twins and Shawn helped with the furniture sale. Jimmy came by to offer his assistance. He also thought he would surprise Pastor by purchasing Autumn's desk. The sturdy piece of oak was far better than the out-dated piece of furniture her Pastor had, ever since the twins were kids. The prices were so good that they sold everything by the early part of the morning—with the exception of a bookcase that she donated to the church.

Autumn had salvaged enough money to pay Sean the interest on her car, pay a few credit card accounts, and have enough money to enter the poker tournament.

Jimmy asked Autumn if she like to ride back to the church and help setup the desk and organize the bookcase. He thought it would be a nice gesture, and Pastor would be thrilled to see her. Somewhat apprehensive, knowing the poker tournament would start in a few hours, she said, "Yes," but she really meant no.

She anticipated getting to the casino to pay Sean his interest and enter the poker tournament.

When they arrived at the church Jimmy reached over the ledge of the door and retrieved the key to open the back entrance to the church. The key had been in the same spot for years. Autumn hadn't been attending services lately, because of her outside activities. When Autumn walked in Pastor's office, she remembered on her last visit to the Pastor; she repaid him the three hundred dollars she had borrowed.

Thinking his money was blessed; she took the borrowed money straight to the casino. She won, but she kept playing never realizing she was a winner until she was broke. Autumn always paid her tithes and offering. Pastor never asked her what the money was for. If she never paid it back it would have been ok. He just gave it to her—no questions asked. The desk and bookcase were as old as the twins. Pastor was very grateful for the fairly new oak desk and bookshelf. It was bigger and better than the old dilapidated ones that the parishioners had given him many years ago.

Gambling

Sean was sitting in his regular seat in the lounge sipping on his cocktail, while waiting for his regular customers to either borrow money or pay the interest on their loan. She quickly paid her interest and proceeded to the cashier's cage.

People were lined up paying the entry fee that was required to play in the poker tournament. Autumn's intentions were that, if she won, she could replace the money she had stolen out of her great-grandmother's bank account, before GG realized the money was gone.

After several hours of playing she made the cut. Autumn had made it to the last table. Regardless if she won the tournament, she wouldn't emerge a loser. Knowing at the moment she had the best hand with a pair of aces, she called all in with the remaining of her chips. To her disbelief, three players called. She lost the hand to three of a kind (three tens).

The captain of the poker tournament gave her a slip to take to the cashier's cage to claim her winnings. The winnings amounted to a few thousand dollars over her entry fee. It still wasn't enough to replace the money in GG's account, but it was a sufficient amount to place another bet.

Although the doors to the firm had closed, the maintenances and utility bills remained. The most important part of the day in Autumn's life consisted of having enough money to catch another poker hand.

Kevin had taken a back seat to her madness. This was not the future he had bargained for. His gambling was more pleasure than addiction. He loved the person he used to know, not the lying, devious, scheming person she had become. Since she basically gambled on the other side of town, he seldom saw her nor did she return his calls. She was caught up in a world of deceit that had no conscience, no morals or values.

The Members Only club card was one of the best investments the twins had made. Autumn tired, broke and hungry had a rich man's appetite and a poor man's bankroll. The Members Only club, with its many vendors, was the place to be.

Every day, there were different vendors with various types of foods and drinks. A person could visit all the booths several times until their tummies were full. This was Autumn's old standby, whenever she ran out of money, or tried to hold on to a dollar. So she could say her favor words "DEAL ME IN."

Confused and baffled with everything coming to a head, not sure of her next move, Autumn struggled with the guilt of stealing her granny's money. The bank wouldn't approve Autumn's application for a loan on her property without her grandmother's signature.

Gambling

The only person that she knew that could help her was her comrade. Missy knew all the underground gold diggers that worked miracles for a buck. They were known as the curb creatures. They would creep out of their holes at night; bite their victim leaving a small-undetected hole in their souls. The victims never realize they have been bitten, until they start dying that slow death caused by stress, drama, fatigue and anxiety.

It was slow in the casino tonight partially due to the weather. The cold, wet climate didn't help business. Most people were at home looking at old movies or doing something constructive.

Autumn was out looking for Missy to introduce her to a curb creature that could give her an illegal loan on the property that she had acquired with the help of her great grandmother.

For some reason, every time she called Missy she would talk for a second and the call would drop. The only part of the conversation she could make out was that Missy was at the casino, ninety miles away, trying to collect on a bad loan.

Hours later, Autumn pulled up in the casino lot, too broke to valet park. She drove around the parking lot looking for a parking space, when she saw two women with the back of their van open, as if they were trying to inhale some fresh air. Next to the van was the only available parking space. Autumn knew the pair would see her. At this point, running out of options, tired and discussed, she could care less who saw her. Brenda greeted her with a "Hey Girl." Autumn replied with a muffled, "Hi." Autumn couldn't believe, once again, the kids were asleep in the back of the van, as if they were at a park or a playground.

Missy seated close to the entrance noticed Autumn, as soon as she walked in. Autumn explained her dilemma and, again, her best friend Missy had a solution to her problem. Tonight she didn't have to make a call to the moneyman. He was seated in the lounge having a cocktail. The curb creature was called Fast Money. He had all the answers. He knew how to forge the deed without GG's knowledge

Autumn knew her friend would take care of business so, this time, she came prepared. She had gone to her safe deposit box earlier to get her deed on the property.

Fast Money owned his own mortgage company, with notary services and a hefty bank account. Autumn a CPA had excellent accounting skills with the lack of street sense. Fast Money loaned her enough to pay off all of her financial responsibility. She knew the papers she signed, that included a balloon payment, were illegal.

GG probably knew by now about the missing money. Autumn put the money back in her granny's account without ever uttering a word. As usual, Missy received her finder's fee, except this time it was so fat, it was in a large brown picture size envelope.

The bonus that Missy had received from her Pay-A-Day loan company and her loan shark friends was enough money to buy herself a three-bedroom home with a loft, a Mercedes, and have money in the bank.

Autumn was so grateful for Missy friendship that she gave her a few hundred dollars for being such a loyal and devoted friend.

All of Autumn's debts were paid. She was back feeling good about life. She gambled night after night winning and losing. The only debt she was accountable for was the loan on her property and her utility bills at her residence.

Months went by, and Autumn's gambling was out of control. Once again she borrowed money on her car to pay her note on the illegal property loan.

Tired from a two-day session of gambling she came home to a cold and musty house. The food in the refrigerator had spoiled from the lack of electricity the house was freezing and the smell of mildew greeted her at the front door. She had forgotten to pay the utility bill.

It was daylight but looking at the clock, she had a few hours before the utility company opened. Within a few seconds she was fast asleep only to be awaken by the loud noise of the garbage truck.

She jumped into the shower, changed her clothes, and ran down the stairs, only to discover that her car was missing. Totally hysterical, she picked up the phone to call the police. As she dialed the number, she quickly hung up, remembering she had not paid the interest to Sean in a couple of weeks.

Sadly, Missy informed her that Sean had repossessed her car for past due interest on her loan. Autumn had no other choice but to get on her two-wheeler and head for the casino! She locked her bicycle in the stall, hoping no one noticed her as she proceeded into the casino. Sean was sitting in his usual seat in the lounge, sipping on a cocktail.

Autumn walked over to Sean with tears in her eyes, pleading with him to give her an extension on the contractual agreement they had made. He said, "Business is business". With the money that she had for her utilities she sat down at the poker table and said, "Deal Me In."

Once again, broke as usual, she called Missy, the only advice her friend Missy could give her was to put her belongings in storage and move in with her. Missy knew with the crooked dealings she encountered, and being a loner, she really didn't enjoy company. But she had made so much money off of Autumn's misfortunes that she felt guilty.

Gambling

Several months had passed Missy was use to her privacy she was tired of sharing her space and money with Autumn. Deep down inside Missy was a very selfish person. She would loan Autumn in hopes that she would win enough money to make other living arrangement or move back to the place she always called home. These days Autumns life was filled with guilt and remorse. The tension was growing more intense by the day. Autumn knew it was time to make other living arrangements. As usual Missy was there to lend a helping hand. She called a friend to assist Autumn with moving her few pieces of furniture to her storage space which housed the rest of her lifetime treasures.

Autumn stood around the casino day after day hoping some of the regulars or lookie loos that she had given money to, back in the day, would reciprocate the favor. It never happened. In the casino, it was a dog eat dog world.

The only tangible item Autumn had left of the life she left behind was on her baby finger. She thought about the pawnshop. She left her bike in the stall and walked across the street only to find the pawnshop was closed—she forgot it was Sunday. The next morning, she was the first customer in line at the pawnshop as they unlocked their doors.

For the twin's sixteenth birthday, great-grandmother had given each of the twins the same, but different colored, rings. Autumn sold her ring for two hundred dollars. Taunted by the thought of her twenty-six birthday next week, she anticipated making enough money to buy back her ring. Autumn then proceeded across the street to the casino and once again said, "Deal Me In."

Chapter 31

THE SHOCK OF HER LIFE

Tired, hungry and disgusted, she mounted her two-wheeler and headed for the Members Only club, where she had dinner, sampling the various foods and visiting the same vendors again and again. Homeless helpless and penniless, she headed for home. Her tired and fragile body reached over the door ledge and retrieved the key to the church, where she had found refuge for the last few months. Once inside her secret hiding place, underneath the pulpit, she sang herself to sleep to the words of "Nobody Knows the Trouble I'm in Nobody knows but Jesus."

At first the flamboyant sound of the choir, the loud movement above her head, as if someone was moving the pulpit, it all seemed like a dream. Trying to wake herself up she realized she wasn't dreaming. She heard the pastor say, "Today we come to honor Sister Helen." Autumn thought, oh my God my GG is getting an award. She was happy for her great grandmother but she felt so remorseful for the life she had chosen and the choices she had made. As the pastor continued to speak, she was in total shock. At this point she realized that the movement above her head was the pallbearers placing her great-grandmother's casket directly over the spot where she had slept and found refuge for the past few months.

Totally distraught as she listened to the eulogy, she laid there crying and urinating on herself all at the same time. In the small surrounding, the guilt and shame that she felt was beyond imagination. She hadn't called home for the last few months never knowing that her great-grandmother had passed away. In total shock, blaming herself for her great-grandmother's death, she laid in the spot under the pulpit for what seemed like days. Trying hard to pull herself together, sipping on a bottle of water, she gathered her bicycle and other belonging out of her secret hiding place.

She rode her bike for hours with nowhere in mind. She felt sick, confused, and somewhat mentally unbalanced. She was on the streets of skid row. People were standing in line as a man passed out meal tickets; it took all the strength that Autumn had to stand in the long soup line that wrapped around the corner. She had been to the mission the previous week, seeking a hot meal and a change of clothing. The streets of skid row brought back many memories. The thoughts of her childhood was very vivid, she could have never dreamed that she would be one of the less fortunate. Feeling dirty, ashamed and guilty, she vowed to herself that if God could forgive her, she would minister to women that had lost their way because of addiction. She prayed that they would learn from her mistakes and not follow in her footsteps. She felt better knowing GG would be proud of her decision to help other women who would fall prey to addictions.

She walked into the mission with her head hanging down. Feelings of guilt, shame and failure had consumed her life. Finally seated at the long table that seated fifty, a lady came over to her table to serve Autumn a bowl of soup and a sandwich. Autumn could not help but notice the lady's hand. The lady had a ring on her baby finger identical to the one that Autumn had sold to the pawn; the only difference was the color. As the twins' eyes met, Amber looked into Autumn's sad and teary eyes and whispered "You Never Realize God Is All You Need Until God Is All You Got."

THE END

www.ingramcontent.com/pod-product-compliance
Lightning Source LLC
Chambersburg PA
CBHW020912090426
42736CB00008B/592